SQUANTO
Friend of the Pilgrims

by CLYDE ROBERT BULLA
Pictures by PETER BURCHARD
Cover by RICHARD WILLIAMS

SCHOLASTIC INC.
NEW YORK • TORONTO • LONDON • AUCKLAND • SYDNEY

To
J. Rowland Whittaker

ISBN 0-590-33937-0

12 11 10 9 8 7 6 5 4 3 2 1   11   5 6 7 8 9/8 0/9

Printed in the U.S.A.   11

CONTENTS

A Ship from Far Away

THE Indian boy lay hidden in the tall grass. Behind him were the woods. Before him were the blue waters of the bay.

Squirrels played in the pine tree above his head. One of them ran down the tree and sat on a low branch near him. The boy could have shot it with his bow and arrow, but he did not move. He looked out across the water at the wonderful sight that was there.

A ship was sailing into the bay. The boy had heard of such ships — bigger than a hundred canoes, with great sails blowing in the wind. Some of the Massachusetts Indians who lived to the north had told him of these ships from far away.

"They are the ships of white men," the Indians had said. "Far to the south the white men have come and built villages. Some day they may come here. They may build villages on the shores of Massachusetts."

The boy had asked his father and mother, "When will I see one of the white men's ships?"

"Maybe never," they had said.

He had watched and waited. He had grown to be almost a man. Now, at last, one of the great ships that had crossed the waters was here.

A shout went up in the woods. He knew that someone else had seen the ship.

The boy wanted to be the first to tell the news in the village. He jumped to his feet and ran.

The village of Patuxet was not far away. It was in a clearing in the woods. There were ten houses in the village. Each one was made of grass mats tied over a frame of poles. There was a field of corn beside each house.

The boy ran through the village.

"White men!" he shouted. "White men have come!"

Faces looked out of doorways.

"Where are they?" asked a girl.

"In the bay," said the boy. "I saw their ship."

He came to his own house. His mother was pulling weeds out of the cornfield. "What are you saying, Squanto?" she asked.

"White men have come," he said. "I saw their ship."

"We had better hide in the woods," said his mother.

"Hide from the white men? Why?" asked Squanto. "I want to see these men. I want to talk with them."

"You could not talk with them," said his mother. "They speak another language. It is a language we do not know."

"Then I could look at them."

"The white men have strange magic," said his mother. "They have fire-sticks that make a loud noise and can kill a bird in the top of a tree."

"I would not be afraid of their fire-sticks," said Squanto. "I want to stay and see these white men."

"Go to your uncle," said his mother. "Ask him what we are to do."

Squanto's uncle was the chief of the Patuxet tribe. His house was the biggest in the village.

Squanto called outside the door. The
chief came out. He was an old man with
deep lines in his face. His long gray hair
was tied so that it hung down his back
like a foxtail.

"The white men have come," said Squanto.

"Did you see them?" asked the chief.

"I saw their ship in the bay."

"They will come here then," said the chief.

"Shall we stay," asked Squanto, "or shall we go away into the woods?"

The old chief said proudly, "I do not fear the white men. If they wish to trade with our people, we will trade with them. Go to your mother, Squanto. Tell her there will be a feast when the white men come to see us. Tell her our men will hunt game in the woods and the women must cook it."

There was great excitement in the village. People talked of the ship in the bay. They talked of the feast.

Hunters went into the woods with their bows and arrows. Squanto went with them. The women built fires in front of their houses.

Before long the hunters were back with the game they had shot. They had ducks, geese, rabbits, and squirrels. One man carried a deer on his back.

Soon the game was roasting over the fires. The children smelled the food. They came close to the fires. "We are hungry," they said.

"Go away," said the women. "This is for the feast."

But when the men were not looking, the women picked off bits of food and gave them to the children.

The men dressed for the feast. Some wore robes of deerskin. Others put feathers in their hair. They painted their faces red, black, and yellow. The chief wore a band of turkey feathers around his head and a string of little sea shells around his neck.

Many families of the Patuxet tribe lived in the woods nearby. When they heard there was to be a feast, they came to the village.

The men grew hungry and ate some of the food. The women and children ate some too.

"Why don't the white men come?" asked Squanto.

"I think they have gone away," said the chief.

"No," said another man. "Their ship is still here, and some of the men came to shore in a little boat. I saw them."

Night came. The fires burned low. The people grew tired of waiting.

Squanto's father and mother went into their house. Squanto went with them and lay down on his bed of grass mats. All over the village he could hear the Indians singing themselves to sleep.

Squanto did not want to sleep. He wanted to stay awake, so he would be sure to see the white men. But his eyes would not stay open. Soon he was asleep.

The Fire-Stick

IT was still dark when Squanto woke. He sat up.

His bed was near the fireplace. The fireplace was a circle of stones on the floor. In the winter his mother cooked on the stones. The smoke went out through a hole in the roof above.

Squanto looked up through the smoke

hole. The sky was growing light. It would soon be morning.

His father and mother were sleeping. He got up without waking them. For his breakfast he took a handful of corn meal from the corn basket. He went outside.

The village was very still. The fires had gone out. Men were sleeping on the ground.

Squanto went down the path toward the shore. He walked beside the little river that ran near the village. He ate the corn meal as he went. He was thinking about the white men. He wanted to know where they were and what they were doing.

When he came to the shore, he saw the great ship in the bay. And he saw something else — a small boat on the sand near the water.

Squanto listened. He heard voices. Quickly he lay down on the ground. He was not afraid, but he remembered what his mother had said: "The white men have strange magic."

He crawled through the tall grass. He crawled up a sand hill and looked over the top. There in the early morning light he saw the white men.

There were nine men sitting around a fire. They all looked very much alike to Squanto. They were covered with clothing so that he could see only their hands and their hairy faces. Even their arms and legs were covered, and they wore shoes that came to their knees. Squanto thought it was strange that they wore so many clothes on such a warm summer morning.

They were eating clams and throwing the shells on the sand. They were talking. Squanto could not understand what they said.

One of the men looked up and said something.

Another one picked up a large black

stick. He pointed it into the air. There was a noise louder than thunder. Smoke and fire came from the end of the stick.

Squanto gave a cry. He jumped out of the grass and fell on his face. He lay there with his hands over his ears.

He heard the white men talking. Someone pulled him to his feet.

He was not hurt. He looked at the fire-stick in the man's hands. Smoke still came from it, but no fire.

Some of the men began to laugh. Squanto looked at them without smiling. He did not like to be laughed at.

The man put the fire-stick under his arm. He walked into the grass and picked up a duck.

Now Squanto saw that the white man had shot the duck with the fire-stick just as an Indian would have shot it with a bow and arrow.

"It made a loud noise," said Squanto. "It hurt my ears, but I am not afraid."

The men looked at each other. They shook their heads. He knew they could not understand him.

One of the men came up to him. He was the youngest of the white men. He said a word that Squanto knew. He smiled and said it again. "Friend."

"How do you know my language?" asked Squanto.

The man pointed to the north. "Massachusetts," he said.

"You learned from the Massachusetts tribe?" asked Squanto.

The man nodded.

Squanto pointed to himself. "I am a Patuxet. I am Squanto."

The man pointed to himself. "Charles Robbins," he said.

It was the strangest name Squanto had ever heard. "Are you the chief?" he asked.

Charles Robbins shook his head. He pointed to the man with the fire-stick.

"Is he the chief?" asked Squanto.

Charles Robbins nodded.

The man with the fire-stick pointed to himself and said, "Captain George Weymouth."

Squanto tried to say it. It was a stranger name than Charles Robbins. He said, "The chief of the Patuxets knows you are here. He waits for you in the village. Come, I will take you there."

He made a sign for the others to follow him.

The white men talked together. Some of them nodded. Some of them shook their heads.

At last Captain George Weymouth, Charles Robbins, and four other men started after Squanto.

Squanto walked very straight. He was happy and excited. He had met the white chief and his men, and they were his friends. Proudly he led them up the path to the village.

Squanto
and the Englishmen

IT was a day of feasting in the village.
More Indians came from their homes in
the woods. More white men came from
the ship.

Captain George Weymouth gave the
chief a present. It was a string of blue
beads. The chief was pleased. He put
the beads around his neck.

He and Captain George Weymouth sat on a deerskin in front of the chief's house. The other white men sat near them.

Some of the Indians said to each other, "These men look very strange."

"They have strange magic," said Squanto's mother. "I wish they would go away."

"They do not mean any harm," said Squanto. "They only want to trade with us."

"I wish they had stayed in their own land," said Squanto's mother, and she went into the house.

An old man of the tribe brought out his drum. He played and some of the young Indian men danced. They made so much dust that the chief told them to stop.

Charles Robbins wanted to play the drum. He tried, but he did not know how. The Indians laughed, and he laughed back at them.

When the feast was over, Squanto walked back to the shore with the white men. He looked at the ship in the bay. He said, "I would like to ride on such a ship."

Charles Robbins said something to Captain George Weymouth. They both

looked at him and nodded their heads.

Charles Robbins spoke to Squanto in the Indian language. "Tomorrow we go." He pointed to the north. "You come?"

Squanto looked at the white men. He looked at the ship. He did not know what to say.

"You come. Tomorrow," said Charles Robbins. Then he and the other white

men got into the small boat. They rowed away toward the ship.

Squanto ran all the way back to the village.

He told his mother and father, "The white men want me to go with them tomorrow. They want me to go on the ship."

His father was pleased. "It is good," he said. "We will tell the chief."

The chief was pleased too. "There is much to learn from the white men," he said. "And you can help them, Squanto, when they trade with other tribes along the shore. You know the language of the tribes. You can talk for the white men."

Squanto went back and forth through the village. He told everyone he met, "I am going on the great ship."

His mother said, "I wish you would not go."

"Why?" asked Squanto.

"Life is good here," said his mother. "The woods are full of game; the sea and the little river are full of fish. There is enough to eat for us all. Our tribe is happy and strong. Why do you want to go?"

"It is for just a little while," said Squanto. "I will come back."

"If you go," said his mother, "I may never see you again."

"Why do you say that?" asked Squanto.

"It is something I feel in my heart," she said.

"Be quiet," said Squanto's father. "It is good that he should go, and the chief wishes it."

Squanto's mother bowed her head and said no more.

In the morning the white men came back. There was trading in the village. The white men traded beads, knives, and cloth for the animal skins the Indians had.

Charles Robbins pointed toward the ship and asked Squanto, "You go?"

"Yes," said Squanto.

The white men took their animal skins down to the shore. Most of the Indians in the village went with them.

Squanto got into the small boat with the white men. They rowed out into the bay.

Squanto looked back at the people on the shore. He saw his father and mother. His mother had her hands over her face. Squanto thought, "She is sad." And he was sad too.

But when the ship sailed, he forgot he had ever been sad. It was an exciting time. The men ran back and forth. They pulled ropes and shouted at each other. Squanto looked at the big sails high over his head. He saw them swell as they caught the wind. He felt the ship move.

It was a wonderful ship, and the white men who had made it were wonderful!

It was true what the chief had said. He could learn many things from them.

As the days went by, the ship sailed up along the shore. Squanto began to learn the language of the white men. He learned that they were English, from the land of England far away.

Charles Robbins told him the names of the days and months. "All the days and months have names," he said. "All the years have numbers. Last year was 1604. This year is 1605."

There were too many names and numbers for Squanto to remember. He wished the white men would not try to teach him so many things at once.

But everyone on the ship was good to him. They spoke kindly to him. They gave him food and clothing. He was proud to think that he could help them. When they stopped to trade with the Indians, Squanto went ahead to each village.

"The white men are coming," he would say. "They are good men and want to be your friends. They have fine things to trade with you, so bring out your best skins to show them."

Charles Robbins told Squanto one day, "We are going back to England soon. The captain would like to take you with us."

"England? Me?" said Squanto.

"We want the people of England to see you. Everyone in England has heard of

Indians, but not many have ever seen one," said Charles Robbins. "You can stay as long as you like and come back on another ship."

Squanto's eyes shone. "Yes!" he said.

He would cross the great ocean. He, Squanto the Indian boy, would be the first of his people to see the land of the white men.

"Yes!" he said again. "Yes, yes!"

London

SQUANTO wanted to go back to his village before the ship sailed. He wanted to tell his people that he was going to the land of the white men.

But the ship was a long way from the village. There was no time for him to go home.

"Talk to the Indians on this shore,"

said Charles Robbins. "Tell them you are going to England. They will talk about it, and the word will get to your people."

Squanto nodded. It was a good plan.

That day he talked to the Indians on the shore. He told them he was going to the land of the white men and would come back soon.

The next day the ship sailed.

At first Squanto was happy. But as the days went by he grew tired of the ocean. He grew tired of eating salt fish and biscuits and beans. He wanted to see land again.

Charles Robbins told him stories to help pass the time. He told him of kings and queens. He told him of the big city of London.

The stories were hard for Squanto to understand. There were so many words in them that he did not know.

Sometimes he was cross because he

could not understand. Sometimes he was sad because there was so much he did not know.

Day after day went by.

One morning a shout went up. "Land!" Squanto and Charles ran up on deck.

"Look, Squanto!" Charles pointed. Far away there was a small dark spot. It was like a little cloud between the ocean and the sky. "It's land! Can you see it?"

"Yes, yes!" said the Indian boy. "I see." And he was happy again.

It was a rainy day in autumn when the ship came in sight of London.

Squanto stood on deck with Charles as they sailed up the river.

"Look at all the ships," said Charles. "They come here from all over the world."

Squanto was not looking at the ships. He was looking at the city. There were so many houses, so close together! And such big houses. There were chimneys everywhere, with black smoke pouring out of them.

The ship passed a great tower rising above high walls. "This is the Tower of London," said Charles. "Long ago the kings of England lived here."

"Oh see!" cried Squanto. "The deer!"

"Deer? Where?" asked Charles. "Oh! They are not deer. They are horses. They are pulling a carriage. And look. There is a man *riding* a horse."

Squanto's eyes were wide. He tried to see everything at once. He began to feel afraid. In such a place, with all its streets and houses, how could he ever learn to find his way?

He kept close to Charles. He was close to him when they left the ship and set foot in the city of London.

He felt strange. The houses and streets seemed to be moving. He took a few steps and fell down.

Charles helped him up. "Don't be afraid," he said. "We are used to walking on the ship. Now it's hard for us to walk on land. We'll have to get used to it all over again. But it won't take long."

People crowded around them.

Someone said, "These men just came from the New World!"

"Did you find gold in America?" asked an old man.

People looked at Squanto. "A savage!" they cried. "An Indian from America!"

They crowded closer. Charles held up his fist. "Out of my way!" He pushed Squanto through the crowd. He pushed him into a carriage and jumped in after him. He shut the carriage door.

The carriage began to move. Two horses were pulling it down the street. A man sat on a seat outside and drove the horses.

Squanto tried to look out the window. He could not see much. Rain was running down the glass.

"We are going to my mother's house," said Charles. "Squanto, do you remember how I taught you to bow?"

Squanto nodded.

"When you meet my mother, bow to her and say, 'Good day, ma'am.' Can you remember?"

Again Squanto nodded.

The carriage stopped before a wooden house with a roof that went up to a point. Charles and Squanto got out and went to the door. Charles knocked.

A woman opened the door. She was

little and old. Her cheeks were pink and her nose turned up.

"Charles!" she cried. "It's you — it's really you!"

Charles went inside. Squanto went in after him.

The woman cried out. "Mercy on us! A savage!"

"Mother, this is Squanto from the New World," said Charles.

Squanto bowed low. "Good day, ma'am," he said.

Mistress Robbins' mouth fell open. "Well! Good day to *you!*" She said to Charles, "He doesn't sound like a wild man. He doesn't look like one either."

"Don't be afraid of Squanto," said Charles. "He is my friend. Be kind to him, and he will be your friend too. And now may we have some food? I am starving. Squanto must be starving too."

Mistress Robbins looked at Squanto. "Does he eat the same things we do?"

Charles laughed. "Try him and see."

They sat down at a table. They had mutton and bread and plum jam to eat and tea to drink. Squanto ate everything on his plate. He could have eaten more, but there was no food left.

Charles told his mother about the New World. While he talked, the room grew dark. The hot tea and the heat of the room made Squanto sleepy. His head began to nod.

"Come," said Charles. "I'll take you to bed."

He took a lighted candle and led Squanto upstairs and into a large room. There was a fireplace in the room. Charles lit the fire.

He opened a chest and took out something that looked like a long white sack. There were buttons down the front.

"Here is one of my old nightshirts," he said. "You can wear it to bed."

He helped Squanto into the nightshirt.

He turned the covers down and Squanto got into bed.

"Go to sleep," said Charles, and he took the candle away.

Squanto curled up in bed. He turned from one side to the other. The pillow under his head was too soft. He pushed it off the bed.

Still he could not sleep. The whole bed was too soft.

He kicked the covers off. He got up and lay down on the floor close to the fireplace. In a little while he was asleep.

The Indian Show

THE next day Charles brought Squanto a soft black hat and a long coat.

"Put these on," he said. "Today we go to see Captain Weymouth. We'll walk over and have a look at London on the way."

Squanto put on the hat and coat. He and Charles went out together. A wind was blowing, and the day was cold. Charles pulled his hat down and turned up his coat collar. Squanto did the same.

"Watch your feet," said Charles, as Squanto stepped in a puddle.

It was hard for Squanto to watch his feet. There was so much to see on every side. He looked at every building they passed.

Charles told him which buildings were homes and which were shops or churches.

Church bells were ringing.

"Oh hear!" said Squanto.

It was like wonderful music.

There were crowds of people on every street. Horses and carriages went by. Children and dogs ran after the carriages.

"Here is the river we sailed up yesterday — the River Thames," said Charles. "Look ahead. Here is London Bridge."

The bridge was like a long street built across the river. On each side of it were houses and shops. Some were new. Some were very old.

"People live here," said Charles. "How would you like to live on London Bridge?"

Squanto thought it would be strange to live on a bridge. He did not think he would like to live in a house with the river running under it.

They walked along the River Thames. They came to the inn where Captain Weymouth was staying.

The captain was glad to see them.

"Everyone knows we are back from America," he said. "They know we have brought an Indian with us. Everyone wants to see him, and I have a plan."

The captain told them his plan. He would rent a hall in the middle of London. In the hall he would build an Indian house. About this house he would put bows, arrows, and a canoe that had been brought from the New World.

"Squanto will sit in front of the house," said Captain Weymouth. "People will pay to come in and look at a real Indian from the New World."

"Do you understand, Squanto?" asked Charles. "Will you do it?"

Squanto nodded, even though he did not understand very well.

By the next week Captain Weymouth had the hall ready. There were bows and arrows on the walls. In a corner someone had built an Indian house of sticks and straw. There was an Indian canoe beside the house. In front of the house sat Squanto.

He was dressed in deerskins, with a band of feathers around his head. There were beads around his neck. His face was painted red and yellow. There were black rings painted around his eyes.

A man stood in the street outside. He rang a bell and shouted, "See the Indian show! Come one, come all! See the real Indian from the New World!"

People paid their money to come into the hall. They looked at Squanto, and he looked at them.

"See the wild Indian!" he heard them say. "Doesn't he look fierce!"

At first Squanto felt proud and important. He liked to think that so many people in London wanted to see him.

But after a while he grew tired of sitting in the hall day after day. When children came to see him they were afraid. Some of them looked at his painted face and began to cry.

Squanto liked the children. He wanted to be their friend. It made him sad to think that they were afraid of him.

Charles saw that Squanto was not happy.

"I know how you feel," he said. "I wouldn't like it either. But the captain is

going away soon. And that will put an end to the Indian show."

Squanto was glad when the Indian show was over. He liked to be at home with Charles and his mother. The big old house was full of wonderful things. He liked to watch the clock and listen to it tick. He thought there must be a little man inside it who made the hands go around.

He liked to look at books with pictures in them. Even the pots and pans in the kitchen were wonderful to him.

Now he was used to his soft bed. He liked to sleep in it. And he liked the food in Mistress Robbins' house — the roasted meats, the jelly tarts, the apple pies, and the puddings made of cream and chestnuts.

Mistress Robbins was kind to him. He wanted to do something for her.

One day he saw a fine brown bird in the yard next door. He ran after it and caught it. He brought it to the door and called Mistress Robbins.

"Oh see!" he said, and he bowed low. "I give bird. For you, ma'am. Thank you, ma'am."

"Where did you get that bird?" asked Mistress Robbins.

He pointed next door.

"Oh Squanto!" she said. "That is one of Mistress Dingle's chickens. You must take it back and tell her you are sorry."

Squanto took the chicken back to Mistress Dingle. "I sorry," he said.

Mistress Dingle laughed. "I know you didn't mean any harm."

Squanto laughed too. He was happy that the people in London were so kind to him. He was happy to be in the land of the white men.

Captain John Smith

ON a spring morning Squanto sat in Mistress Robbins' front yard. Birds were singing. The grass was green.

There was an elm tree in the yard. Squanto looked up into it. He thought of the trees at home and the woods where he used to play. He thought of the village and his father and mother.

He went into the house. He said to Charles and Mistress Robbins, "I go, please."

"Go where?" asked Charles.

"Home," said Squanto.

"Mercy on us!" said Mistress Robbins. "Do you want to leave us so soon?"

"Don't you like London?" asked Charles.

Squanto tried to tell them that he did like London. He liked it very much. But he had been here many, many days. It was time for him to go home. He wanted to be with his people again and tell them of the wonderful things he had seen.

"I understand," said Charles. "I'll find out when the next ship is going to the New World."

But not many ships were going to the New World. The few that were going had no room for Squanto.

He waited, and the months went by.

Charles went to sea again. He was gone a year. When he came back, Squanto was still there.

"I don't know what I would have done without him," said Mistress Robbins. "In the summer he worked in my garden. In the winter he brought in wood and kept the fires going. He kept me from being so lonely too."

"I'm glad you were here, Squanto," said Charles. "I'm glad you could stay with my mother. But you still want to go home, don't you?"

"Yes, please," said Squanto.

"I'll try to find a way for you," said Charles.

For a long time he tried. He talked to his friends and to the sea captains he knew. But he could find no one to take Squanto back to the New World.

Months passed, and years. Squanto began to think he could never go home again.

Then a visitor came to see him.

It was on a day in autumn. Squanto was burning leaves in Mistress Robbins' front yard. A man rode up on a fine black horse. He jumped down and tied the horse to the fence.

He wore a long cloak and a hat with a plume. His beard almost covered his face. He asked, "Are you Squanto the Indian?"

"Yes sir," said Squanto.

"I am John Smith," said the man. "Captain John Smith. I've come to see you. Can we sit here and talk?"

They sat on the front step together.

"I know your friend Charles Robbins," said Captain Smith. "He tells me that you are from Massachusetts Bay, near Cape Cod."

"Yes sir," said Squanto.

"Tell me about it," said Captain Smith. "Tell me everything you can think of."

Squanto told him about the shore and the trees. He told him about the fish in the sea and the animals in the woods. He told him about the people of the Patuxet tribe.

Captain Smith listened to every word. "You have told me things I wanted to know," he said. "I have been to America and I am going again. I am going to

Massachusetts to make maps for the king."

"Take me!" said Squanto. "Oh please!"

"There may be a place for you on my ship," said Captain Smith. "I'll see."

Squanto was excited.

He told Charles and his mother, "I go home — yes, yes!"

But as time went by, he thought Captain Smith had forgotten him.

Then Charles came home with the news.

"I saw Captain Smith today," he said. "He is going to take two ships to America in the summer. There will be room for you on one of them."

"Oh, glad day!" cried Squanto. "Captain Smith not forget. No, no! Now I go to my people. Now I go home!"

Captain Hunt

IN the summer of 1614 the two ships sailed for the New World. John Smith was captain of one. Thomas Hunt was captain of the other.

Thomas Hunt was a little man with a sharp tongue. Squanto did not like the sly look on his face. He was glad he was not on Captain Hunt's ship. He was glad to be with Captain Smith instead.

Once a storm drove the ships far apart, but most of the time they were in sight of each other.

One day they sailed into a rain. When the rain stopped they could see land.

"Oh see!" cried Squanto. He watched the land ahead.

"What will your people do when you come home?" asked Captain Smith. "Will they have a feast in the village?"

"Big feast," said Squanto. "You come?"

"No, Squanto," said Captain Smith. "We will land many miles north of your home. My men and I are going to explore along the shore. We want you to come with us."

"I go home," said Squanto.

"But will you come with us for just a day or two?" asked Captain Smith. "You can help us meet the Indians. You can help us talk to them."

Squanto nodded. "Yes," he said. "I help."

The two ships sailed into a port. The men landed. They made camp on the shore. They caught fish and shot wild turkeys and cooked them over big fires.

In the morning the two captains said good-bye to each other. Captain Hunt and his men sailed south to look for furs and codfish. Captain Smith and his men went north to explore and make maps of the country.

Squanto went with Captain Smith. They found an Indian trail and followed it to a village.

Squanto spoke to the Indians. He told them the white men were their friends. For two days they feasted together. Then Squanto said to Captain Smith, "I go home."

"Yes, Squanto," said Captain Smith.

"Go to your people now. Go home and be happy there."

They said good-bye. Squanto went down the trail and into the woods.

It was a three days' walk to Patuxet village. Squanto thought how surprised his father and mother would be to see him again. He thought how excited everyone in the tribe would be.

There would be a feast. All the tribe would sit around him. He would tell them about the land of the white men.

He sang as he walked through the woods. He sang the songs his people had taught him long ago.

Squanto slept under a tree that night. Early in the morning he was on his way again.

He came to the ocean. Not far from shore was Thomas Hunt's ship.

While Squanto looked at it, Thomas Hunt and six of his men came out of the woods. They came toward him.

"I thought you went with Captain Smith," said Thomas Hunt.

"He go north," said Squanto. "I go home."

Captain Hunt pointed to the south. "Is your home that way?"

"Yes," said Squanto.

"Stay with us," said Captain Hunt. "We are going to sail south in a day or two. You can sail with us."

"No," said Squanto. "I go."

The men looked at Captain Hunt. He said something to them in a low voice. He and the men came closer.

"Wait," said Captain Hunt. "Will you eat with us before you go?"

The words were friendly. But there was a sly look in Captain Hunt's eyes that made Squanto draw back.

"I go now," he said.

As he started away, two of the men caught his arms. They threw him down upon the sand.

Squanto kicked and fought. He nearly got free. Then all the others leaped upon him. They pushed his face into the sand. At last he lay still.

He heard Captain Hunt say, "Get the ropes out of the boat."

Someone tied his arms and legs together.

Two of the men stood him on his feet.

"What you do?" cried Squanto. "Why you do this to me?"

"Bring him along, men," said Captain Hunt.

Two men dragged him across the sand. There was a small boat at the edge of the water. They pushed him into it and rowed away.

When they came to the ship, someone let a rope down over the side. One of the men tied the rope under Squanto's arms. He felt himself being pulled up to the deck.

"What you do?" cried Squanto.

No one spoke to him. Two sailors dragged him down one stairway and then another. They opened a small door in the floor. It was the door to the hold in the bottom of the ship.

The sailors let Squanto down through the doorway. He heard the door fall shut above his head.

In the Dark

SQUANTO lay in the bottom of the ship. It was dark in the hold. Only a little light came in around the door above.

Something moved in the darkness. Someone spoke. "Who is there?"

It was a man, and he spoke in the Indian language!

Squanto answered in the same language, "Who are you?"

"I am Wawano," said the man.

"I once knew a man named Wawano," said Squanto. "Are you of the Patuxet tribe?"

"Yes," said the man.

"Then you are the man I knew!" said Squanto. "Do you remember Squanto?"

"Yes," said the man. "Long ago he went with the white men. He never came back."

"He did come back," said Squanto. "He is here. I am Squanto."

He told Wawano of his years in England. He told him how he had come back with Captain John Smith. "I was going to my village when I met Captain Hunt. He and his men tied me and brought me here." Squanto asked, "Can you take the ropes off my arms and legs?"

"No. I am tied too," said Wawano. "Yesterday I saw the white men on the shore. They were fishing, and I went to help them. They threw me down and tied me with ropes and brought me here."

"We have done them no harm," said Squanto. "Why have they done this to us?"

"I do not know," said Wawano.

"I cannot stay here," said Squanto. "I must go to my people. Tell me of my father and mother, Wawano."

"They are old," said Wawano. "They talk of you. They say they will never see you again."

"I must go to them!" said Squanto. "Help me get free!"

But there was no way for Wawano to help him.

The next day Squanto heard a noise above his head. There were footsteps and loud voices. He looked up. He thought someone had come to set him free.

The door opened above. Men began to drop down into the hold. Squanto could hear them falling all about him. He could hear them shout and groan.

The door closed. The men called to each other in the dark. They were all shouting and talking at once. They all spoke in the Indian language.

Squanto and Wawano talked with them. The men told their story. There were twenty of them, all of the Patuxet tribe. They had come to trade with the white men. They had brought their furs to the ship. The white men had taken them prisoner and tied them with ropes.

"Why are we prisoners?" cried one of the men. "What have we done?"

"What will the white men do with us?" asked another. "Where are they taking us?"

Squanto could feel the ship moving. If only the ropes were off his arms and legs, he could set all the others free. They could run up to the deck, jump into the ocean, and swim to shore.

He twisted and turned, but he could

not get free. The ropes were too tight and too strong.

That night the door opened. Someone put down a ladder.

A little sailor came down the ladder. He had a lantern in one hand and a kettle of food in the other.

Beside each Indian he put a biscuit and a salt fish.

He went up the ladder and came back with a pail of water and a pan. He set the pan on the deck and poured the water into it.

"Why you do this to us?" asked Squanto.

The little sailor did not answer. He went back up the ladder.

The Indians could not use their hands. They had to eat the food off the deck. When they drank, they had to roll over to the pan and put their faces into the water.

Every night the little sailor brought

food and water. Every night Squanto asked him, "Why you bring us here? What place you take us to?"

At last the little sailor told him, "I didn't want to do it. Some of the others didn't either, but we had to do what the captain said. The captain is taking you across the ocean. He is going to sell you there."

"*Sell* us?" said Squanto.

"Yes," said the little sailor. "You are going to be slaves."

The Slave Market

AFTER a few days the Indians were chained to the walls of the hold. They could walk only a little way, but they could stand up and lie down, and their hands were free.

Sometimes they were quiet for hours. Sometimes they talked a little and tried to see one another's faces in the dark.

"Is it day or night?" they would ask one another.

Sometimes they talked of the white men.

"They are bad!" said Wawano.

"All white men are not like Captain Hunt," said Squanto. "Many white men are good. I know, because I lived among them."

Some of the Indians wept when they talked of their homes and their people. But they never let the white men know they had wept.

When the white men brought food and water, the Indians looked at them with proud faces. They would not answer when the white men spoke to them.

The little sailor told Squanto, "Captain Hunt is going to bring all the Indians up on deck for an hour every day. He says it is bad for you to stay all the time in this dark place."

Squanto told the others what the little sailor had said.

"Captain Hunt cares nothing for us," said Wawano. "He is afraid we will be sick and he cannot sell us for such a good price."

Squanto was one of the first to be taken up on deck. It was good to see the sky again. It was good to breathe the fresh air.

But it hurt him to see the ocean all around him. There was no land in sight. He thought how near his village had been and how far it was now.

For many weeks they sailed. They came in sight of land where the hills were green and the sun was bright and warm.

The little sailor told Squanto, "This land is Spain."

They sailed along the shore and into

a port. On the port was a city of white walls and low houses.

The little sailor told Squanto, "This city is Málaga."

The next day the Indians were tied with ropes again. They were tied so that they could stand up and walk.

Captain Hunt and his men led them off the ship and into the city. People on the streets stopped to look. Some of them were men in long brown robes.

Squanto heard two of Captain Hunt's sailors talking.

"See the Brothers in their brown robes," said one.

"Who are they?" asked the other.

"They are good men of the church," said the first sailor.

Captain Hunt's men and the Indians came to a square in the middle of Málaga. All about the square were markets where many things were sold. There were ducks, geese, and chickens for sale. There were fish. There were shoes and cloth and lace and flowers. In one corner of the square was the slave market.

The Indians were taken to the slave market. Men crowded around to look. They nodded their heads as if they were pleased.

An Indian was lifted up on a wooden block. One of the men quickly bought him and paid his money to Captain Hunt.

One by one the Indians were sold and led away.

Even before Squanto was put up on the block, men were bidding for him. He could hear them shouting. He could see their faces turned up toward him.

He looked away. To one side he saw two men. They were looking at him as if they were sorry for him. He saw the brown robes they wore. He knew that they must be good men of the church.

A man with gold rings in his ears

pulled Squanto off the block. He poured a bag of money into Captain Hunt's hands and led Squanto across the square.

Squanto saw the two men still looking at him.

He broke away from the man who had bought him. He ran as fast as he could with the ropes on his legs. He threw himself down before the men in the brown robes.

"Oh help!" he cried. "I no be slave. No, no! Oh help, please!"

The men looked down at him. "English!" said one of them. "He speaks English!"

The man with the gold earrings came running after Squanto. He saw the two men and stopped.

Squanto lay still. He heard the voice of the man who had bought him. He heard the voices of the other two men. They talked for a long time.

He could not understand the language. He never knew what was said. But at last the man who had bought him went away.

The men in brown robes helped Squanto to his feet.

"Come," said one of them. "You are free."

The two men called themselves Brother Luis and Brother Diego.

Brother Luis could speak English. He talked to Squanto as they walked through the streets.

"Where is your home?" he asked.

"America — far across sea," said Squanto.

They climbed a hill to a church high above the city. Behind the church was a square of small white houses. In front of the houses were gardens and fruit trees.

"Welcome," said Brother Luis. "Welcome to our home."

Christmas Eve

SQUANTO was not strong after the long weeks on the slave ship. The Brothers put him to bed and cared for him. They kept a dish of oranges and grapes by his bed.

In a few days he was well enough to sit outside in the sun. In a few more days he was helping the Brothers work in their gardens.

He watched the ships in the port. He

said to the Brothers, "You help me go home, please?"

An English ship came into the port. Brother Luis went down to talk with the captain.

He came back and told Squanto, "The captain will take you with him if you want to go."

"Oh yes!" said Squanto.

"He is not going to the New World," said Brother Luis. "He is going to London. But in London you will have a better chance to find a ship that will take you home."

So Squanto said good-bye to the Brothers. He left Málaga on the English ship.

It was Christmas Eve when the ship reached London. Bells were ringing. The London streets were white with snow.

Squanto walked through the streets to Mistress Robbins' house. There was a light in the window.

He knocked. A woman came to the door. He had never seen the woman before. He bowed and said, "Mistress Robbins, please."

"She's not here," said the woman.

"Charles Robbins, please," said Squanto.

"They are both gone," said the woman.

"When they come back?"

"They aren't coming back," said the woman. "They moved away."

"Where?" asked Squanto.

"I don't know," said the woman, "and I can't stand here talking all night. The house is getting cold."

She shut the door.

Squanto stood on the step. The wind was sharp and cold. The snow blew into his face.

He began to walk to keep warm. He walked past inns where people were eating and drinking. He was hungry, but he had no money to buy food.

On a corner he saw a big stone house. There were lights in all its windows. Through the windows he could see people laughing and dancing.

He knew that it was warm inside. He knew that there must be food in the kitchen.

He went up to the house and knocked.

A little girl opened the door. A little boy peeped out from behind her.

"Oh!" said the girl. "Did you come to our Christmas party?"

"No," said Squanto. "I cold. I come in, please?"

"I'll have to ask my father." The girl ran into the room where the people were.

Squanto heard a woman call, "John! John Slanie! Come here. Your daughter wants you."

Then he heard the little girl say, "Father, there's a gypsy at the door."

The little boy smiled up at Squanto. "Do you want to see my toys?" he asked.

The girl came back. A man was with her.

"Here is the gypsy, Father," she said.

The man looked at Squanto. "Why, this is no gypsy. This is — Squanto!"

"How you know my name?" asked Squanto in surprise.

"Do you remember a long time ago

when you were in the Indian show? I went to see you. After that I used to see you on the streets of London. Why are you here?" asked the man. "Did you want to see me?"

"I cold. I hungry," said Squanto.

"Let him come in, Father," said the girl. "You will, won't you?"

The man led Squanto inside and shut the door. The boy brought a ball, a wooden soldier, and a toy sheep for Squanto to see.

"I think my children like you, Squanto." The man said to the boy, "Would you like to take Squanto to the kitchen? Tell the cook to give him something to eat."

"Will the cook give me something to eat too?" asked the boy.

"She may, if you ask her," said the man. "After you eat, bring Squanto back to me. We will find him a place to sleep tonight."

John Slanie's House

SQUANTO slept in one of the servant's rooms back of the kitchen.

On Christmas morning John Slanie talked with him.

"I heard that you went back to the New World," he said. "How does it happen that you are here?"

Squanto told him what had happened.

The girl and boy, Anne and Edward, sat near him and listened.

He told of Captain Hunt and the slave ship and of the Brothers in Spain.

"Captain Hunt is a bad man," said Anne. "If I ever see him, I'll tell him so."

"But I like the Brothers," said Edward. "They were good men."

"It may be that I can help you get home," said John Slanie. "I am a merchant. I buy and sell goods from all over the world. Some day I may send a ship to America to trade with the Indians. But it may be a long time."

"I wait," said Squanto.

John Slanie was a very rich man. His house and stables were large, and he kept many servants.

Squanto became one of his servants. He kept the stables clean and he helped care for the horses. John Slanie had twelve horses — four to ride and eight to pull the carriages.

Almost every day Anne and Edward came out to see Squanto. He told them stories of America. He made a bow and arrow for Edward.

"I don't want you to go to America," said Edward. "I want you to stay here."

"Shame on you!" said Anne. "Squanto wants to go home. How would you feel if Mother and Father were all the way across the ocean and you couldn't go to them?"

"Well, I didn't mean forever. Of course I hope Squanto can go home some day," said Edward, "but I want him to stay here a long time first."

Squanto did stay a long time. For more than three years he was a servant at John Slanie's.

The cook told him of a band of people who were going to the New World to live.

Squanto asked John Slanie about them. "Do you know these people?"

"No, but I have heard of these poor pilgrims," said Slanie.

"Pilgrims?" asked Squanto.

"I call them pilgrims because they wander here and there. They have no real homes," said Slanie. "The king will not let them have their own church in England. Many of them have gone to Holland, but they are not happy there. They want to go to the New World where they can live and be free."

"I go with pilgrims?" asked Squanto.

"Maybe there will be a better way," said Slanie. "I know of a ship that may go to America this year. The captain wants to take someone who knows the country — "

"I know country!" said Squanto.

"Would you guide the captain?" asked Slanie. "Would you help him trade with the Indians?"

"Yes, yes!" said Squanto.

"I'll send the captain to see you," said John Slanie.

The captain came to see Squanto. His name was Thomas Dermer. He talked with Squanto about America.

"You take me home?" asked Squanto.

"Yes," said Captain Dermer, "but you must help me first."

"I help. Yes, yes!" said Squanto.

He was happy. He sang at his work.

"You're glad!" said Edward. "You're glad because you're leaving us!"

"No," said Squanto. "I glad because I go home."

Home

LATE in the year 1619 Captain Dermer's ship sailed for America.

The captain said to Squanto, "Take your last look at England."

Squanto looked for the last time at the land of the white men. Then he turned his face toward America.

Captain Dermer sailed straight across

the ocean. He landed in the New World on an island far north of Squanto's home.

He sailed from place to place. He and his men caught fish. They traded with the Indians.

Squanto led the way through the woods. He went with the white men to the Indian villages. He helped the white men and Indians talk with each other.

He kept asking Captain Dermer, "I go home now?"

"No," the captain would say. "We need you here."

The ship sailed down along the shore. By summer it was loaded with animal skins and salt fish to take back to England.

The captain made ready to sail back across the ocean. He and Squanto said good-bye to each other.

Four of the sailors took Squanto to shore in a small boat. They landed near Cape Cod, not far from his village.

They waved good-bye as they rowed away. He waved back.

He felt a little lonely as he stood there on the shore. But he thought, "This is my home. My people and my village are here."

He walked through the woods. It was good to feel the grass under his feet. It was good to smell the leaves and feel the cool wind on his face.

He came to a trail that led to the village. There was something strange about the trail. Grass had grown over it, as if no one had used it for a long time.

Something else was strange. He had walked for miles, yet he had seen no one.

Just ahead was the clearing he knew so well. He could hear the river that ran by the clearing.

He began to run. He ran out into the clearing, and there he stopped.

The village was gone.

He looked all about him. He went to

the place where his house had been. Among the weeds and grass he found an old broken bowl. That was all.

What had happened to the village? Where were his people? Why had they gone away?

He left the clearing. He walked along the river. He looked for someone who could tell him where his people had gone.

He walked on and on. When night came he lay down on a bed of leaves.

In the morning he met a young Indian hunting in the woods.

The hunter started to run away.

"Stop!" called Squanto in the Indian language.

The Indian stopped. He came slowly back. "You wear the white man's clothing. I thought you were a white man," he said. "Who are you?"

"I am Squanto. For a long time I have lived with the white men. Yesterday I

went back to the place where my village used to be. What has happened to Patuxet village? Where are the people who lived there?"

"The Patuxets?" said the hunter. "There are no Patuxets."

"I am a Patuxet," said Squanto.

"Then you are the only one," said the hunter. "Two summers ago there was a great sickness among them. It took everyone in the tribe."

"No!" cried Squanto. "It cannot be true."

"It is true," said the hunter. "They could do nothing to stop the sickness. If you had been there, it would have taken you too."

Squanto went away into the woods, where he could be alone. He leaned against a tree and closed his eyes.

"My people!" he whispered. "My people and my village — gone! There is nothing left for me."

For a long time he stood there.

The young hunter came up behind him.

"Squanto," he said, "come."

"Where?" asked Squanto.

"To my village," said the hunter. "It is not far. My chief is Massasoit. He and the rest of the tribe will welcome you."

He started away. He looked back. "Squanto, will you come?"

"Yes," said Squanto, "I will come."

The Pilgrims

THE young hunter's name was Ocomo.
He led Squanto to his village. It was a
large village beside a bay.

Chief Massasoit came out of his house
to meet Squanto. He was a young chief,
tall and strong, with long black hair.
Others came to look at the strange Indian
in white man's clothing.

"Who are you?" asked Massasoit. "Where is your home?"

"I am Squanto, the last of the Patuxet tribe, and I have no home," said Squanto. He told his story. "Now I have no people. I have nowhere to go."

"You are welcome here," said Massasoit.

Ocomo took Squanto to his home in the village. It was a small house. He lived there with his mother, father, and three brothers.

Squanto tried to be happy in the home of Ocomo. But he had lived with white men so long that Indian ways were strange to him. Indian food and clothing were strange too.

At night the small house was crowded. Squanto's bed was hard. All about him the Indians sang themselves to sleep. Their singing kept him awake.

In the village lived a young chief named Samoset. He had come from the north to visit Massasoit. He had known many white hunters and traders. They had taught him some words of the English language.

Samoset liked to talk to Squanto about the white men.

He said to Squanto one day, "You must hunt and fish with the others. You must play games with the men of the tribe. Then you will not be so sad."

Squanto hunted and fished with the others. He tried to join in the games. But he felt no better.

He was weary of the village. He was weary of the people in it.

One day he heard two men talking about him.

"Here comes Squanto," said one.

"Let's get away," said the other, "before he starts to tell one of his long stories about the white men."

Then they laughed.

Squanto was hurt because they

laughed at him. He was angry too. He went away into the woods. For many days he hunted and fished alone.

He built a little house of poles and the bark of trees. Snow came and covered it, and it was warm under the snow.

Winter was almost over when Ocomo came to his house.

"We have looked for you," he said.

"Why?" asked Squanto.

"We want you to come with us," said

Ocomo, "when we go to talk with the white people."

"The white people?" asked Squanto.

"Yes," said Ocomo. "We do not know whether they want to be friends or not."

"Where are these people?" asked Squanto.

"Their ship is in the bay where the Patuxet village used to be," said Ocomo. "All winter the ship has been near the shore. The white men came to the shore. Then they went back to the ship. Many times they did this, as if they did not know where to go. We hid in the woods and watched them. But now they have come to stay."

"How do you know?" asked Squanto.

"They are building houses," said Ocomo. "They have women and children with them."

"The Pilgrims!" said Squanto.

"Pilgrims?" said Ocomo.

"They are people who want to have their own church and be free," said Squanto. "I heard of them in London. When I left the white men's land, they were making ready to come here. I know they must be the same people!"

"At first we kept away from them," said Ocomo. "Some of our people feared their magic and wished to drive them away. But Samoset said they would do us no harm. He went to visit them. They gave him gifts and wanted to see the chief. Massasoit is going to visit them. He wants you to go too."

"I will go," said Squanto.

They started back together. Early the next day they reached the village.

Massasoit was ready to visit the white men. His face was painted red. He wore a deerskin on his shoulders. About his neck was a string of white bone beads.

Most of the other men of the tribe

were going with the chief. They had painted their faces and put on beads and their best animal skins.

"See!" said Samoset, when Squanto came into the village. "See what the white men gave me."

He was wearing his presents — a bracelet, a ring, a knife, a pair of shoes and stockings, a green shirt, and a black hat.

"We are glad you have come, Squanto," said Samoset. "You can talk to the white men better than I."

They started up the trail. They walked in a long line. Some of the women and children walked beside them.

All day they walked, and at night they made camp.

Early in the morning they went on. It was still morning when they came to a hill where strawberry vines grew thick in the summer. On the other side of the hill was the river that ran into

the bay. On the other side of the river the Pilgrims had built their houses.

The chief said to Samoset and Squanto, "Go and tell them we wait here."

Samoset and Squanto waded across the river to the village of the white men. It was a small village. There was one large house with walls made of mud. There were a few huts made of mud and sticks.

"Part of this village is where Patuxet village used to be," said Squanto.

A dog began to bark.

The door of the large house opened. A short little man with red hair came out. Other men came running. All had fire-sticks in their hands.

"Friends!" called Squanto. "We are friends!"

Slowly the men put down their fire-sticks.

The red-haired man came forward.

"Where do you come from?" he asked. "How did you learn to speak English?"

"I live in England many, many years," said Squanto.

"Then you must be the Indian I've heard about," said the red-haired man. "Is your name Squanto?"

Squanto was pleased. "I am Squanto, yes, yes!" He pointed to the hill across the river. "Chief Massasoit waits there. He will talk to your chief."

"I am Captain Miles Standish," said the red-haired man. "Tell your chief to

come here and we will talk to him."

Word was carried back and forth from Captain Standish to the chief.

At last Chief Massasoit, with twenty of his men, came to the white men's village.

The chief sat in one of the houses with the white men's governor, John Carver.

Outside the house the Indians and white people looked at one another. They did not know what their leaders were saying. They did not know whether they would be friends or not.

Inside the house the chief and the governor talked. Squanto sat near them.

He spoke in the English language to Governor Carver, "Chief Massasoit say his tribe do no harm to white men. He say when Indians come they leave bows and arrows behind."

He spoke in the Indian language to Chief Massasoit, "The governor tells me the name of this village is Plymouth.

He wants you to know the people of Plymouth will do no harm to the Indians. When they visit the Indians they will leave their fire-sticks behind."

"It is good," said Massasoit. "Our people will be friends."

He and the governor came out of the house together. They were smiling.

The Indians and white people knew that they were to be friends. They began to nod and smile at one another. They shook one another's hands.

There was a day of feasting. The next day Massasoit and his men started back to their village.

Squanto went with them to the river.

The other men waded across. They looked back at him.

Samoset called, "Are you coming, Squanto?"

Squanto shook his head. "I stay," he said.

Plymouth

A small boy came down the street of Plymouth and stood by Squanto.

"Where are the Indians going?" he asked.

"Home," said Squanto.

"Why don't you go?" asked the boy.

"I stay here," said Squanto.

"You won't get much to eat," said the boy.

"Why?" asked Squanto.

"Because we don't have much," said the boy. "We didn't have much before the Indians came, and they ate nearly all we had left."

A woman came out of one of the houses. "John!" she called.

"That's my mother," said the boy. "She's calling me." But he did not go. "You come with me and I'll show you everything. See that ship out there?"

"Yes," said Squanto.

"That's the *Mayflower*," said the boy. "We all came across the ocean on that ship. In a little while the *Mayflower* is going back to England. Then we will be here alone."

"John! John Billington!" called the woman.

"See that big house?" said the boy. "It's the first one we built. We all slept in it at first, but now most of us have our own houses."

A little girl looked out of one of the houses.

"She is Ellen More," said the boy. "She is afraid of you, but I'm not."

A man came out of the big house. He was young and tall. He looked very strong.

"Here comes John Alden," said the boy.

"Go to your mother, Master Billington," said the man. "Do you not hear her calling?"

The boy made a face and went away. He met another boy. The two began to play leapfrog.

"I am glad the children can play sometimes," said John Alden. "There is little play for the rest of us. We have fields and gardens to plant and more houses to build. There are a hundred of us to feed. Some of us should be in

the woods now, hunting for food."

"Fish in river," said Squanto. "Why you not fish?"

"To tell the truth," said John Alden, "we have no hooks for fishing."

"You have nets?" asked Squanto.

"No," said John Alden.

Squanto went away. He went down

the river bank. With his bare feet he began to tramp on the mud at the edge of the water.

John Billington looked down over the bank.

"What are you doing?" he asked.

Squanto kept on tramping. A long, fat eel popped out of the mud. Squanto caught it and threw it to the boy. "Eels swim up river," he said. "They hide in mud. I know where."

He tramped out another eel.

"Can we eat them?" asked John Billington.

"Yes, yes," said Squanto. "Take to your mother."

He climbed up the bank. He saw some of the men digging in the earth with hoes. They were planting corn.

"No, no!" he said.

The men looked up.

"You plant too close," said Squanto. "Look — do this way. Dig hole. Put in seeds — one, two, three, four, five. Put fish around seeds. One, two, three fish."

"Fish?" said one of the men. "What for?"

"Fish make earth good," said Squanto. "Make corn grow high."

"How can we get fish?" asked the man.

"Fish in river," said Squanto. "We catch fish with nets. We make nets of grass. I show you."

He went down to the shore where the grass was tall and strong. John Billington went with him. The little girl, Ellen More, walked behind him. She was not afraid of him now.

As they pulled the grass, Squanto looked up the hill at the village of Plymouth. These Pilgrims were brave, he thought. They had come to the New World where everything was strange to them. They did not know how to live here. They did not know how to hunt, fish, or grow corn. He, Squanto, would show them. He would be a friend to these people. He would never leave them.

He looked up at the pine trees about him. When he was a boy he had played under these trees. "This my home again," he said.

"What did you say?" asked John Billington.

"This my home," said Squanto.

"Were you talking to the trees?" asked John Billington. "That's foolish, if you were. A tree doesn't know what you are saying."

But the little girl put her hand in Squanto's, as if she understood.